Introduction to Contract Law in India

Siva Prasad Bose

Published by Joy Bose, 2022.

Introduction to Contract Law in India

By Siva Prasad Bose

Published by Joy Bose

Copyright © 2022 Siva Prasad Bose

Contents

Dedication

This book is dedicated to the constitution of India, which is the source from which all laws in India derive.

Preface

Contracts are a part of our everyday lives, whether we realize it or not. From buying groceries to signing employment agreements or engaging in e-commerce transactions, contracts form the legal foundation of countless interactions. This book aims to provide a clear, accessible, and practical introduction to contract law in India, making it especially valuable for students, professionals, and anyone seeking to understand the legal framework governing agreements.

In this book, we discuss what is a contract, the history of contract law and the important laws in India that govern contracts, namely the Indian contract act and the sale of goods act. We also discuss the conditions for a valid or invalid contract, the elements of a contract and some special types of contracts.

We begin by explaining what a contract is, including its essential elements and historical development. From there, we cover fundamental doctrines such as offer and acceptance, consideration, free consent, and capacity to contract. Special emphasis is given to real-world concerns like fraud, coercion, undue influence, and misrepresentation—concepts that often determine the enforceability of contracts.

Major statutory frameworks such as the Indian Contract Act, 1872 and the Sale of Goods Act, 1930 are discussed in detail, alongside practical legal concepts like quasi-contracts, warranties, and vicarious liability. We also delve into modern dimensions of contract law, including digital contracts, online consumer rights, and the increasing importance of electronic communication in forming agreements.

To support learning and application, the book includes sample contract templates and a glossary of key legal terms. Each chapter is written in a straightforward style, with examples and case law to reinforce understanding.

It is hoped that this book will serve as a useful and practical guide for anyone seeking to understand contract law in India, and will empower readers to navigate legal agreements with greater confidence and clarity.

Acknowledgements

While writing this book, we have gone through the following sources related to contract laws:

LexisNexis. Mulla. The Indian Contract Act by Dindhaw Fardunji Mulla. Edition 2021

Encyclopedia Britannica. Contract law. https://www.britannica.com/topic/contract-law

John D Calamari and JM Perillo. Contracts. Black Letter Outlines, Fifth edition. Thomson Reuters.

Chapter 1: What is Contract Law?

In this chapter, we will discuss the concept of contracts and contract law in brief.

1.1 What is a contract

A contract is a voluntary agreement between two or more persons to exchange something of value, called consideration. It confers certain rights and imposes certain obligations to the parties making the contract, which are enforceable by law. Both the parties mutually and freely intend to and agree to enter into the contract. In a contract, each person is legally bound to do what is promised. A party who fails to live up to the agreed promise has breached the contract.

The contract may be oral or written or executed through electronic communication such as email or fax. It may be explicitly stated or implicitly agreed via the conduct of the parties involved.

When we agree to buy something, we essentially form a legal contract. For example, A buying a bar of soap from B upon making a payment of Rs 10 is a contract of sale, even though there may not be any formal written documentation or oral statement of the contract. The law of contract is relevant for many parts of our daily life, and it is important to understand contracts in order to protect ourselves as consumers.

A contract between two parties is marked with one party making an offer and the other party giving their acceptance to the offer. The offer made may alternatively be rejected by the other party, or a counteroffer made, whose acceptance will create another legally binding contract.

Contract law deals with the definition of a contract, elements of a contract, validity and duration of the contract, the consequences if any party breaks the contract and similar issues. In India, contract law is served by the Sale of Goods Act 1930 and by the Indian Contract Act 1872.

The following are all different types of contracts

- Agreement for sale
- Agreement for exchange
- A cheque
- Warranty
- Transfer of shares
- Employment agreement containing details of salary package, working hours, and work responsibilities

For example, suppose A has an item for sale. B makes him an **offer** to buy the item for a certain price X. The next step can be any one of the following:

- **A accepts B's offer without any conditions**. The acceptance is communicated to B. It becomes a valid contract and A has to sell the item to B at the agreed price X.
- **A makes a counteroffer** to B to sell the item at a slightly higher price Y. If B accepts the counteroffer, then it becomes a valid contract.
- **A rejects B's offer**. Then there is no contract.
- Before B's acceptance and the communication of the acceptance to A, **A revokes the offer** or it **lapses** after a time limit mentioned in the original offer. Then there is no contract.

After the contract is agreed, A has to sell the item to B at the agreed price. If A fails to deliver the item after the contract is in place despite

B paying the price, or does not fulfill any other expressly stated or implied term of the contract, it becomes a **breach of contract**. B can then sue A in a court of law for remedies related to the breach of contract. The court may order remedies such as **damages** that A must pay to compensate B for the breach. The amount of damages is typically calculated by taking into account A's loss incurred from the **nonperformance** of the contract, and to restore the state if the contract had been performed as originally agreed. Another possible remedy the court can order is **specific performance**, i.e., the court can order A to fulfill his obligation as part of the contract.

1.2 Meaning of contract

According to Section 2(h) of the Indian Contract Act, a contract is "an agreement enforceable by law." An agreement, as per Section 2(e), is "every promise and every set of promises forming consideration for each other."

Thus, for an agreement to be a contract, it must be enforceable by law.

The meaning of contract, taken from different sources, is as follows:

- An agreement enforceable by law is a contract: Indian contract Act 1872
- An enforceable covenant or agreement between two or more persons with a lawful consideration or course (Tomlin)
- From dictionary of finance and investment: Contract in general is an agreement by which right or acts are exchanged for lawful consideration. To be valid, it must be entered into by competent parties, must cover a legal and moral transaction, must possess mutuality and must represent a meeting of minds. Countless transactions in finance and investments are covered by contracts.
- While it is probably impossible to give an absolute and

universally correct definition of a contract, the most accepted definition is a promise or a set of promises which the law will enforce. The expression "contract" may be used to describe any or all the following:

a. the series of promises or acts themselves constituting the contract
b. the document or documents constituting the contract
c. the document or documents constituting or evidencing that series or promises or acts or their performance
d. the legal relations resulting from that series

(Halisbury, 4th edition, Vol. 9, para 201, p80)

Contracts have been divided, according to the mode of their function, into three classes:

- Contracts of record
- Contracts under seal
- Simple contracts

1.3 Essentials of a Valid Contract

The key elements of a valid contract include:

- Offer and Acceptance
- Intention to Create Legal Relationship
- Lawful Consideration
- Capacity to Contract
- Free Consent
- Lawful Object
- Certainty and Possibility of Performance
- Not Declared Void

Each of these essentials is discussed in greater detail in subsequent chapters.

1.4 Types of Contracts

Contracts may be classified based on various criteria:

(a) Based on Validity:

- Valid Contract
- Void Contract
- Voidable Contract
- Illegal Contract
- Unenforceable Contract

(b) Based on Formation:

- Express Contract
- Implied Contract
- Quasi Contract

(c) Based on Performance:

- Executed Contract
- Executory Contract
- Unilateral Contract
- Bilateral Contract

1.5 Legal Framework for Contracts in India

The Indian Contract Act, 1872 is divided into two main parts:

- **Part 1 (Sections 1 to 75)**: General Principles of the Law of Contracts
- **Part 2 onwards**: Special kinds of contracts, such as contracts relating to indemnity, guarantee, bailment, pledge, and agency

1.6 Scope and Application

The Indian Contract Act applies to all Indian states except Jammu & Kashmir (now subject to changes post-Article 370). It is applicable to both citizens and foreign nationals, and governs commercial and civil contracts across sectors.

1.7 Principles Underlying Indian Contract Law

Indian contract law is based on several foundational principles:

- **Pacta sunt servanda** (agreements must be kept): contracts are binding and enforceable.
- **Freedom to contract**: parties are generally free to decide the terms of their agreement.
- **Good faith and fair dealing**: although not always expressly required, fairness is often implied.
- **Remedies are compensatory, not punitive**: courts award damages to compensate loss, not to punish.

These principles ensure predictability and fairness in contractual dealings.

1.8 Role of Judiciary in Contract Law Development

Indian courts have played a vital role in shaping contract law. Landmark judgments by the Supreme Court and various High Courts have clarified ambiguities, refined principles, and adapted the law to modern realities.

For example:

- In *Mohori Bibee v. Dharmodas Ghose* (1903), the Privy Council clarified that a contract entered into by a minor is void.

- In *Kedar Nath v. Gorie Mohammad* (1886), the court elaborated on enforceability of promises with consideration.

1.9 Emerging Areas in Contract Law

Contracts form the foundation of business relationships. With the rise of digital transactions, e-contracts, and cross-border agreements, understanding contract law is more relevant than ever. Awareness of one's rights and duties under contract law helps prevent disputes and ensures legal compliance.

With the changing nature of commerce and technology, new domains of contract law are developing:

- **E-Contracts**: Formed via digital platforms, including 'clickwrap' and 'browsewrap' agreements.
- **Smart Contracts**: Blockchain-based self-executing contracts coded with conditional logic.
- **Cross-border Contracts**: Agreements involving parties from multiple jurisdictions requiring clarity on governing law and dispute resolution.

1.10 Importance of Understanding Contract Law for Laypersons

Understanding basic contract principles is vital for:

- Protecting one's rights in daily transactions
- Evaluating terms before signing agreements (e.g., job offers, lease agreements, service terms)
- Recognizing what constitutes a breach and when legal recourse is possible

Even simple exchanges—such as a service booking, online purchase, or family loan—can involve legal obligations.

1.11 Conclusion

This introductory chapter outlines the basic definition, scope, and types of contracts. In the following chapters, we explore each element of a valid contract in detail, along with illustrative examples and case law.

Chapter 2: History of Contract Law

In this chapter, we will discuss briefly the history of contract law and its evolution. Having a climate where well-defined contract laws exist and are protected by the state is essential for commerce to flourish in a country.

2.1 Contract Law in Roman Times

Roman law, codified by emperor Justinian in 6th century AD, had the concept of contracts.

They had three components of a valid contract, namely, the thing which is contracted, the price of the thing and agreement or consent between the parties. The agreement could be in verbal or written form.

Roman law also allowed for different kinds of contracts including sale-purchase, hire, partnership between two or more people and mandate or acting upon instructions. All types of contracts were enforceable by the law.

2.2 Contract law in the Middle Ages

In Europe in the Middle Ages, the contract law survived in an elementary form. However, around 13th century as trade began to develop in Italian city states and elsewhere, the mercantile courts arose to resolve disputes between merchants on the basis of contract law.

2.3 Contracts under English common law

The English common law is a system of laws that arose in England which was based on precedents or previous judgments of English courts on similar types of cases, rather than based on principles as in

European law. Law in India is also mainly part of the common law system, due to the Indian legal system being modelled on the English common law system during the British rule, and many Indian laws such as the Indian Contract Act being formulated by the British based on similar laws in England at that time, which have continued to be applicable even after India's independence with a few modifications.

English common law has the concept of debt, relating to a fixed sum of money owed that was recoverable, and the concept of covenant, relating to a promise made. In modern times, the common law version of contracts included offer, acceptance, consideration and the voluntary and mutual intent between the parties to be bound by the agreement.

2.4 Contracts under Canon law of the church

The Canon law of the catholic church in Europe during the Middle Ages also had a version of contracts. It had the notion that promises should be binding or *pacta sunt servanda* in Latin.

2.5 Contracts under Islamic law

Islamic law also had the notion of contracts. Under Islamic law, there were four elements of a contract namely the buyer, seller, subject matter of the contract (*maqud alayh*) and the form of the contract (*sighah*) comprising offer and acceptance. In India and the Arab world amd trading routes such as the silk route, an informal system of value transfer called the hawala system developed in the Middle Ages.

2.6 Contracts in British India

British India resulted in development of a court system based on common law, similar to the system in England. The main law governing contracts was the Indian Contract Act 1872.

2.7 Evolution of Contract Law in Post-Independence India

After India gained independence in 1947, the Indian judiciary began adapting contract law to Indian socio-economic conditions. The courts interpreted the Indian Contract Act in light of constitutional values, especially those in Articles 14 (equality) and 21 (life and liberty). The growth of consumer rights, industrial regulation, and public interest litigation has also influenced how contracts are viewed and enforced.

Important judicial decisions have clarified principles such as free consent, unconscionable contracts, and standard form contracts. For example, the Supreme Court in *Central Inland Water Transport Corporation Ltd. v. Brojo Nath Ganguly* (1986) invalidated unfair contract terms that violated public policy and natural justice.

2.8 Contract law in other countries

UK and its former colonies such as US, Canada and Australia follow the common law system, based on the legal precedents made by various courts.

In particular, different states of the USA may have a different set of precedents and hence slightly different versions or interpretations of the law. US follows a Uniform Commercial Code or UCC. Its contract law is based on the principles of an offer and acceptance of the offer, consideration for the offer and promissory estoppel which is the cause of action to decide when the contract is breached.

European countries like Germany generally follow the civil law system which is derived from the Roman law that was propounded by Emperor Justinian. Different countries in Europe have a common set of model rules called the Principles of European Contract Law (PECL), on which the contract laws of the individual countries are based.

2.9 Impact of Globalization and Technology

With economic liberalization in the 1990s, Indian contract law had to respond to globalization and digital commerce. Contracts are now commonly formed through email, websites, mobile apps, and digital signatures. Courts have generally recognized these as valid modes of contract formation, provided legal formalities are followed.

International trade and foreign investment have increased reliance on cross-border contracts, leading to greater consideration of international principles such as those in the UNCITRAL Model Law on Electronic Commerce and international arbitration frameworks.

2.10 Conclusion

The history of contract law in India reflects a blend of ancient customs, colonial legal heritage, and modern legal developments. From oral traditions and religious texts to digital contracts and cross-border agreements, the evolution of contract law mirrors the economic, social, and technological growth of India. The next chapter will explore the concept of offer and acceptance, one of the foundational pillars of any contract.

Chapter 3: Offer and Acceptance

———

In this chapter, we explore the foundational concepts of offer and acceptance, which form the starting point of any valid contract. A contract comes into existence only when one party makes an offer and the other party accepts it.

3.1 Meaning of Offer

An offer is a proposal by one person, called the offeror, to another person, called the offeree, indicating a willingness to do or abstain from doing something with a view to obtaining the other's assent.

As per Section 2(a) of the Indian Contract Act, 1872:

"When one person signifies to another his willingness to do or to abstain from doing anything, with a view to obtaining the assent of that other to such act or abstinence, he is said to make a proposal."

For example, if A says to B, "I will sell you my bicycle for ₹2,000," A is making an offer to B.

3.2 Essentials of a Valid Offer

- The offer must be communicated to the offeree.
- The offer must be certain and definite.
- The offer must show the willingness of the offeror to be bound.
- It must be made with an intention to create legal obligations.

3.3 Types of Offer

- **Express Offer**: Clearly communicated in words (spoken or

"

written).

- **Implied Offer**: Inferred from conduct or circumstances.
- **General Offer**: Made to the public at large (e.g., reward advertisements).
- **Specific Offer**: Made to a particular person or group.
- **Cross Offer**: Two identical offers made by parties in ignorance of each other's offer.
- **Counter Offer**: A reply to an offer which introduces new terms and amounts to rejection of the original offer.

3.4 Acceptance

Acceptance is the act of giving assent to the offer. Section 2(b) of the Indian Contract Act defines acceptance:

"When the person to whom the proposal is made signifies his assent thereto, the proposal is said to be accepted."

Once the offer is accepted, it becomes a promise.

3.5 Legal Rules Regarding Acceptance

- Acceptance must be absolute and unqualified.
- It must be communicated to the offeror.
- It must be in the prescribed mode, or a reasonable mode.
- Silence does not amount to acceptance.
- Acceptance must be made while the offer is still open.

3.6 Communication and Revocation

As per Sections 3 to 5 of the Indian Contract Act:

- Communication of offer is complete when it comes to the knowledge of the offeree.
- Communication of acceptance is complete:

- ◦ As against the proposer: when acceptance is put into transmission.
  - ◦ As against the acceptor: when acceptance comes to the knowledge of the proposer.
- Revocation of offer or acceptance must happen before the communication is complete.

3.7 E-Contracts and Online Offers

In the age of digital commerce, offer and acceptance often happen through email, websites, or apps. Clicking "I Agree" or placing an online order is considered valid acceptance under law. The Information Technology Act, 2000 supports the recognition of electronic records and signatures in such contracts.

3.8 Case Laws

- **Carlill v. Carbolic Smoke Ball Co.** (1893): A general offer made to the public was held to be valid and enforceable when accepted by use.
- **Felthouse v. Bindley** (1862): Silence was held not to constitute acceptance.
- **Harvey v. Facey** (1893): A mere statement of lowest acceptable price is not an offer.

3.9 Conclusion

Understanding offer and acceptance is crucial to recognising when a valid agreement is formed. The communication and timing of these actions determine whether a contract exists. In the next chapter, we shall examine the concept of consideration, another key requirement for a valid contract.

Chapter 4: Indian Contract Act 1872

In this chapter we discuss the Indian Contract Act, which is the principal law in India that governs contracts. It was brought by the British rulers of India at that time and is based on similar laws in use in Britain.

4.1 Introduction to the Indian Contract Act 1872

THE INDIAN CONTRACT ACT, 1872

ACT No. 9 OF 1872[1]

[*25th April*, 1872.]

Preamble—WHEREAS it is expedient to define and amend certain parts of the law relating to contracts;

It is hereby enacted as follows:—

PRELIMINARY

1. Short title.—This Act may be called the Indian Contract Act, 1872.

Extent, Commencement.—It extends to the whole of India [2][except the State of Jammu and Kashmir]; and it shall come into force on the first day of September, 1872.

Saving—[3]*** Nothing herein contained shall affect the provisions of any Statute, Act or Regulation not hereby expressly repealed, nor any usage or custom of trade, nor any incident of any contract, not inconsistent with the provisions of this Act.

2. Interpretation-clause.—In this Act the following words and expressions are used in the following senses, unless a contrary intention appears from the context:—

(*a*) When one person signifies to another his willingness to do or to abstain from doing anything, with a view to obtaining the assent of that other to such act or abstinence, he is said to make a proposal;

---

1. For the Statement of Objects and Reasons for the Bill which was based on a a report of Her Majesty's Commissioners appointed to prepare a body of substantive law for India, dated 6th July, 1866, *see* Gazette of India, 1867 Extraordinary, p. 34; for

Figure: First page of the Indian Contract Act 1872

The Indian Contract Act 1872 is the main act that defines the contract law in India. It states the circumstances in which a contract between two or more parties can be enforced in Indian law.

4.2 Elements of a Contract as per Indian Contract Act 1872

A legally binding contract must have the following elements, as per the Indian contract act 1872:

- **Offer**: There must be an offer by one party. An offer is a promise to be bound if certain specific terms are accepted unconditionally by the other party. The offer may be made to a specific person, to a class of people or to the world.
- **Acceptance**: The offer must be accepted by the other party. The law infers acceptance from certain actions, such as signing a contract or beginning to carry out the terms of a bargain.
- **Promise**: When the offer is accepted, it becomes a promise, which is legally enforceable.
- **Promisor and Promisee**: The person who makes the promise is called the promisor. The promise must be directed to a specific person, who accepts the promise and is called the promisee.
- **Consideration**: This refers to the price paid for the promise. In every valid contract, there must be an exchange of consideration. this means that something of value is given for something else of value. For example, if A buys a blouse at a store, A's consideration is the money being paid and the merchant's consideration is the item being bought. The value of the two items does not have to be the same, and law allows consumers to make both good deals and bad deals. As per the Indian Contract Act, a valid consideration exists when "*When at the desire of the promisor, the promisee or any other person has done or abstained from doing, or does or abstains from doing, or promises to do or abstain from doing something*".
- **Agreement**: The promises made along with the consideration for the promise is called the agreement.
- **Contract**: An agreement enforceable by law is a contract.
- **Void contract**: A void contract is a contract that is not enforceable by law.

- People entering into a contract must be legally competent to make contracts. For example, they cannot be mentally ill or intoxicated, or less than the minimum age for contracts.
- **Performance**: This refers to the fulfilment of obligations by the parties as part of the contract.
- **Termination of a contract**: A contract can be terminated or discharged upon performance of the obligations, by mutual agreement between the parties, by lapse of time as per the Limitation Act, by death, insolvency, or alterations in the contract, or by breach of the contract.
- **Breach of contract**: It is caused due to failure in performing the obligations by any party. The affected party can sue the party committing the breach in the court. Remedies available include damages, termination of the contract, specific performance of the contract or other remedies such as injunctions or restoration to the status quo. Damages are typically awarded by the courts in such a way so as to restore the state as if the contract had been performed.

4.3 Types and Conditions for a valid offer as per Indian Contract Act

The offer can be of different types such as:

- express offer, that is made expressly in writing or through speech.
- implied offer which is understood by the conduct of the parties.
- general offer to the public or a specific offer to a party
- continuous offer kept open for a time
- counteroffer made by the person who is offered initially.

The conditions for a valid offer are as follows:

- The offer should be in certain terms and not vague.
- The offer may be written, spoken or implied.
- The offer may be general to all members of the public, or specific to a person
- The offer may be continuous or time bound, with a fixed expiry time
- The offer must be communicated.
- The offer should not just be a statement of intention.
- The offer may be revoked before acceptance, but once accepted it becomes legally binding.
- The offer can be rejected, either expressly or implied.

4.4 Acceptance as per the Indian Contract Act

The rules for acceptance of a contract as per the Indian Contract Act are as follows:

- **Absolute and unqualified**: Acceptance of an offer by a party should be absolute and unqualified. For example, there should not be a counteroffer by the party to buy the items at a different price than that one offered
- **Communicated**: The acceptance should be communicated to the party making the offer, in a written or verbal form.
- **Mode**: Acceptance must be in the mode prescribed. If not, the offerer may inform the same to the person accepting the offer that the acceptance is not as per the prescribed mode such as writing or verbal or email.
- **Time frame**: The acceptance must be made within a specific time frame and before the offer is lapsed.
- **Acceptance after offer**: The acceptance can only be after an offer is made, not earlier.
- Silence by one party cannot be held as acceptance.
- Acceptance must be given expressly by speech or in writing, or

else implied by the actions of the acceptor of the offer.

- Acceptance should be of all the terms of the offer, not just some of the terms.

4.5 Lawful consideration as per the Indian Contract Act

The rules for lawful consideration as per the Indian Contract Act include the following:

- The action should be at the desire or request of the promisor. If the action has been made without the promisor expressly requesting for it, then no consideration is payable.
- The consideration must be real and not illusory.
- The consideration must be having some value as per law.
- Consideration may be in the past, present or future.
- Consideration may move from the promisee to another person.
- Consideration need not be adequate or equal in value to something given. All that is necessary is that it should have some value.

The rules for unlawful consideration are as follows:

- Consideration must not be something that the promiser is already bound to do.
- Consideration should not be forbidden by law
- Consideration should not involve injury to any person
- Consideration should not be immoral, fraudulent, or opposed to public policy

4.6 Persons competent to make contracts as per the Indian Contract Act

The persons competent to make a contract include the following:

- The person should not be a minor as per law.
- They should not be bankrupt.
- They should not be of unsound mind when making the contract, such as mentally ill or intoxicated.
- They should not be disqualified by law from making the contract, such as being a convict, or alien enemy.
- They should be making the contract out of their own free will and consent, and not be subject to coercion, undue influence, fraud or misrepresentation.

4.7 Performance as per Indian Contract Act

Performance of a contract is the fulfilment of the obligations. Performance can be immediate or delayed or time bound, can be performed by one party or be reciprocal, and can be demanded by the party to whom the obligation is promised or by their heirs or legal representatives.

Section 37 of the Contract Act states as follows: *Obligation of parties to contract.—The parties to a contract must either perform, or offer to perform, their respective promises, unless such performance is dispensed with or excused under the provisions of this Act, or of any other law. Promises bind the representatives of the promisors in case of the death of such promisors before performance, unless a contrary intention appears from the contract..*

4.8 Agency

As per the law, the contracts can be made either between the two parties directly, or by the persons (the agents) who are legally authorized and competent to act on behalf of the parties (the principals).

The agency can come to an end in any of the following ways:

- If the principal revokes the agency of the agent
- If the agent themselves renounce their agency
- If the business of the agent is completed
- If the principal is declared insolvent.

4.9 Amendments and Repeals

Since its enactment in 1872, the Indian Contract Act has undergone several amendments. Originally, the Act had 266 sections, but over time, several parts relating to contracts concerning partnership, contracts relating to sale of goods, and contracts relating to negotiable instruments have been carved out into separate laws:

- The Indian Partnership Act, 1932
- The Sale of Goods Act, 1930
- The Negotiable Instruments Act, 1881

Presently, the Indian Contract Act is mainly divided into two parts:

1. **General Principles of the Law of Contracts** (Sections 1 to 75)
2. **Special kinds of contracts** including:
    - Contracts relating to indemnity and guarantee (Sections 124–147)
    - Contracts relating to bailment and pledge (Sections 148–181)
    - Contracts relating to agency (Sections 182–238)

4.10 Relevance in Contemporary Times

Despite being enacted over 150 years ago, the Indian Contract Act continues to remain relevant and forms the backbone of commercial and personal legal transactions in India. With the rise of digital commerce, online contracts, and international trade, courts have interpreted and applied its provisions to suit modern contexts.

Judicial decisions have ensured that the Act evolves through interpretation and case law to cover electronic contracts, consumer protection, standard form contracts, and the doctrine of unconscionability.

4.11 Key Case Law Interpreting the Act

Some important judgments that have shaped the application of the Indian Contract Act include:

- *Mohori Bibee v. Dharmodas Ghose* (1903): Held that a minor's agreement is void ab initio.
- *Carlill v. Carbolic Smoke Ball Co.* (1893): Though an English case, it is frequently cited in Indian law for principles of general offer and acceptance.
- *Balfour v. Balfour* (1919): Clarified the principle that social/domestic agreements do not typically have legal enforceability.
- *Central Inland Water Transport Corporation v. Brojo Nath Ganguly* (1986): Struck down unconscionable clauses in employment contracts as being against public policy.

4.12 Comparison with International Principles

The Act is broadly based on English common law principles, but with uniquely Indian elements. With growing globalisation, Indian contract law is increasingly compared with international frameworks like:

- UNIDROIT Principles of International Commercial Contracts
- United Nations Convention on Contracts for the

International Sale of Goods (CISG)
- English Law of Contract

These comparisons help in harmonising dispute resolution, especially in cross-border agreements where parties choose Indian law as the governing law.

4.13 Conclusion

The Indian Contract Act, 1872, remains one of the most enduring pieces of legislation in India. It continues to guide commercial, civil, and increasingly digital transactions. Its clear structure, supported by evolving judicial interpretations, makes it a foundational pillar of Indian civil law.

In the following chapters we shall discuss some specific cases related to the act in more detail.

Chapter 5: Free Consent – Coercion, Undue Influence, Fraud, Misrepresentation and Mistake in Contracts

In this chapter we discuss the conditions that constitute fraud, coercion or undue influence in a contract. If any of these conditions are proven, the contract can be voided.

5.1 Fraud in a contract

Some definitions of fraud from dictionaries and judgments are as follows:

- Fraud is an act of deliberate deception with the design of securing something by taking unfair advantage of another. It is the deception in order to gain by another's loss. It is a cheating intended to get an advantage [SP Chengalvanya v Jagannath AIR 1994 SC 853].
- Fraud arises out of a deliberate active role of representation about a fact which he knows to be untrue, yet he succeeds in misleading the representee by making him believe it to be true. The representation to become fraudulent must be of fact made with the knowledge that it was false [Shristi v Shaw Bros. AIR 1992 SC 1555].
- Fraud is a false misrepresentation by one who is aware that it was untrue with an intention to mislead the other who may act upon it to his prejudice and to the advantage of the representator [State of Maharashtra v Buddhikota AIR 1989 SC 2292].

- Webster's third New International Dictionary - Fraud in equity has been defined as an act or omission to act or concealment by which one person obtains an advantage against conscience over another or which equity or public policy forbids as being prejudicial to another.
- Black's law dictionary – fraud is defined as an intentional perversion of truth for the purpose of inducing another in reliance upon it to part with some valuable thing belonging to him or surrender a legal right; a false representation of a matter of fact whether by words or conduct, by false or misleading allegations, or by concealment of that which should have been disclosed, which deceives and is intended to deceive another so that he shall act upon it to his legal injury.
- Halisbury laws of England – a representation is deemed to have been false and therefore a misrepresentation, if it was at the material date false in substance and in fact.

Although it is not exactly correct to say that fraud must be proved with strictures of a criminal charge, there is no doubt that a very high degree of proof is needed to establish it [William and Mortimer 16th Ed p 173].

Fraud, in all cases, implies a willful act on the part of anyone whereby, another is sought to be deprived by illegal or inequitable means, of something which he is entitled to [Green v Nixon (1857) 23 Bear 530].

Fraud has been defined in Section 17 of the Contract Act which is but an explanation.

Fraud is either actual or constructive. Actual fraud is sub divided into two parts:

- misrepresentation and

• concealment.

Misrepresentation (called *suggestio falsi*) must be of a material fact and must have been relied or acted upon by the person deceived.

Concealment (called *suppresio veri*) is the suppression or withholding of some material fact, being some fact which one party was under the legal duty to the other to disclose [Turner v Green (1895) 2 CH 205, AIR 1953 SC 163, AIR 1956 MB 246, 249].

Effect of fraud: the effect of fraud on any processing or transaction is that it becomes a nullity. Even the most solemn proceedings stand vitiated if they are actuated by fraud. Such being the nature and consequence of it, the law requires not only strict pleading of it but strict proof as well.

If fraud is proved in a contract, the affected party can make it void, or apply for damages from the party that committed fraud, or can insist of the performance of the original contract.

5.2 Coercion in a contract

Compulsion by physical force or threat of physical force, conduct that constitutes the improper use of economic power to compel another to submit to the wishes of one who wields it [Black's Law Dictionary].

Coercion takes an infinite number of forms, but it may properly be thus defined: the moment that the person who influences the other does so by the threat of taking away from that other something that he then possesses, or by preventing him from obtaining an advantage he would otherwise have obtained, then it becomes coercion and ceases to be persuasion or consideration [Ellis v Barker (1871) 40 LJ Ch 603/607].

Coercion is defined by Section 15 of the Contract Act 1872 as "the committing or threatening to commit any act forbidden by law (IPC) or the unlawful deterring or threatening to detain any property to the prejudice of any person whatever with the intention of causing any person to enter into an agreement." It is the first portion of the definition which would properly apply. To constitute undue influence in the eyes of the law, there must be coercion.

Examples of coercion are as follows:

- Threat to commit suicide is coercion [AIR 1969 Cal 293].
- Coercion in Section 72 of the Contract Act must be understood in the ordinary sense. In includes every kind of compulsion even if it does not measure up to the definition under Section 15 of the Contract Act [AIR 1969 MYS 230]

5.3 Undue Influence in a Contract

Undue influence is the improper use of power or trust in a way that deprives a person of free will and substitutes another's objective [Black's Law Dictionary: 8th Edition].

Undue influence includes any influence in which the exercise of free and deliberate judgement is excluded. Undue influence is presumed until the contrary is proved when the relation of the parties is such that one is entitled to the confidential advice of the other, as in the case of solicitor and client, of a trustee and trust and of a parent contracting with a child who has first come of age. In other cases of confidential relationship, the party seeking to avoid a contract must prove undue influence [Sutton and Shannon on Contracts 6th Edition].

Every influence cannot be characterized as undue. A done can appeal and persuade the donor to make a gift to him. Such appeals and persuasions cannot be characterized as undue influence, provided the donor retains the mental capacity [Takri Devi v Rama AIR 1984 HP

11, 15, Subhas v Ganga Prasad AIR 1967 SC 878, Afsar v Solamn AIR 1976 SC 163].

Undue influence as defined in Section 16 of the Contract Act 1872, is that relation which subsists between the parties by which one of the parties is in a position to dominate the will of the other and uses that position to obtain an unfair advantage over that other [AIR 1996 Ker 64, AIR 1956 MB 246, AIR 1960 Cal 551, AIR 1979 SC 1431, Barry and Butler – AIR 1976 Cal 377, AIR 1955 SC 363, AIR 1968 SC 964].

5.9 Distinction Between Coercion and Undue Influence

- **Nature**: Coercion involves physical or unlawful threats, while undue influence involves moral or mental pressure.
- **Relationship**: Coercion can be used by anyone, but undue influence usually involves a fiduciary or special relationship.
- **Effect on Consent**: Both vitiate free consent, but the remedies and presumptions may vary.

5.10 Burden of Proof

- In cases of coercion or fraud, the burden lies on the person alleging it.
- In undue influence, if a fiduciary relationship is proved, the burden may shift to the dominant party to show that the contract was fair and not influenced by the relationship.

5.11 Remedies for Contracts Induced by Coercion or Fraud

- **Rescission**: The contract can be declared voidable at the option of the aggrieved party.
- **Restitution**: The aggrieved party is entitled to be restored to the position before the contract.

- **Damages**: In cases of fraud, damages may also be claimed for losses suffered.

5.12 Fraud in the Digital Era

With the rise of online transactions, new forms of fraud such as phishing, identity theft, and fraudulent e-commerce have emerged. While the Indian Contract Act remains applicable, courts may refer to the Information Technology Act, 2000 for enforcement and evidence.

Online platforms often use terms and conditions to limit liability, but such clauses may not be enforceable if entered under coercion, undue influence, or deception.

5.13 Case Law Highlights

- *Ranganayakamma v. Alwar Setti* (1889): Consent obtained during the performance of funeral rites was held to be coercion.
- *Muthia v. Karuppan* (1927): Presence of a fiduciary relationship gave rise to a presumption of undue influence.
- *Derry v. Peek* (1889): Established that fraud requires false representation made knowingly or without belief in its truth.

5.14 Conclusion

The principle of free consent is central to the enforceability of contracts. Coercion, undue influence, fraud, and misrepresentation all affect the validity of an agreement. With the evolving landscape of contracts—including digital agreements—understanding the boundaries of free consent is essential to protect legal rights and prevent exploitation.

Chapter 6: Void, Voidable and Unenforceable Contracts

In this chapter we discuss the conditions that make a contract invalid or unenforceable as per the Indian contract act. If these rules are met, then the contract is considered void or it cannot be enforced.

6.1 Difference between void, voidable and unenforceable contracts

A void contract is something that is legally not a valid contract at all, and the parties are not bound by it.

A voidable contract is a contract which, depending on some conditions, can be voided or its terms can be set aside by one of the parties.

An unenforceable contract is a contract which is not enforceable i.e., if any party does not do their performance agreed under the contract, they cannot be compelled to do so.

6.2 Conditions for void contracts

Agreements to do something illegal or something that is against public policy are not enforceable in the courts and are hence considered void. For example, an agreement to sell illegal drugs.

Fraud and misrepresentation are grounds for invalidating a contract. An example of a fraud is a false statement to induce one party to agree to a contract. Misrepresentation can be in the form of either making a misleading statement or intentionally withholding information in a statement that could have caused the party to not agree to the contract.

Some other types of void contracts are as follows:

- **Mistake of fact**: If there are mistakes in the contract that are factually wrong, that can make it void.
- **Mistake of law**: If the consideration or the object of the contract is illegal, that can make the contract void. However, part of the contract may still be valid.
- **Agreements without Consideration**: A contract without consideration is void.
- **Agreements in restraint of trade**: A contract that restrains trade are void since they infringe on the free choice of the persons.
- **Agreements in restraint of marriage**: Such agreements are also void since they infringe of person's freedom, these apply for contracts that restrain the right of a person to marry another.
- **Agreements in restraint of legal proceedings** are also deemed void.
- **Uncertainty or Impossibility of performance**: Contracts involving actions that are impossible to perform are also deemed as void.
- Agreements related to wagers and bets are also deemed as void.

6.3 Conditions for unenforceable contracts

A minor person usually cannot enter into a contract. E.g., a person under the age of 18 (and sometimes 21) is a minor and therefore cannot enter into a contract. Contracts involving minors are usually unenforceable, as the minor cannot be compelled to the performance under its terms.

A contract that is unfair e.g., which favors a particular party may be found unfair and unconscionable, and hence unenforceable in the court if the following conditions are met:

- the consumer is presented with a contract on a take it or leave it basis.
- there is uneven bargaining power between the parties, such as when the seller is educated and experienced and the consumer is uneducated.

Some types of work bonds, such as a promise to work in an IT company for a certain number of years or to never work for a competitor, may also be unenforceable.

6.4 Voidable contracts

Some contracts are voidable, means they can be rendered void by any of the parties. Until they are rendered void, they remain valid and enforceable. This includes cases such as the following:

- **Lack of free consent**: This may happen where one of the parties may not have given consent out of free will. Therefore, if one of the parties can prove they were coerced into making the contract, they can choose to void it.
- **Prevention of performance by the other party**: If it is proved that the other party has prevented the party from fulfilling its performance obligations then the contract can be voided by the party which was prevented.

6.5 Distinction Between Void and Voidable Contracts

Criteria	Void Contract	Voidable Contract
Validity	Not valid from the beginning	Valid until rescinded by the aggrieved party
Legal Effect	No legal enforceability	Enforceable until voided
Cause	Illegal object, uncertainty, etc.	Coercion, fraud, misrepresentation, etc.
Remedy	Not enforceable by either party	Aggrieved party may rescind or enforce

6.6 Unenforceable Contracts in Practice

Unenforceable contracts may arise due to technical defects such as:

- Absence of a required stamp or registration
- Lack of written documentation where mandated
- Expiry due to limitation period

Though valid in substance, these cannot be enforced unless formal defects are cured.

6.7 Legal Consequences and Remedies

- **Void Contracts**: No party can claim damages. However, restitution under Section 65 of the Indian Contract Act may be allowed.
- **Voidable Contracts**: The aggrieved party can claim damages and cancel the contract.
- **Unenforceable Contracts**: Once defects are rectified (e.g., through stamping), such contracts can become enforceable.

6.8 Judicial Interpretations

- *Mohori Bibee v. Dharmodas Ghose* (1903): Minor's agreement held void ab initio.

- *Kanhaiyalal v. D.R. Banaji* (1958): Explained difference between void and voidable.
- *Gherulal Parakh v. Mahadeodas* (1959): Discussed the scope of public policy in declaring contracts void.

6.9 Conclusion

In this chapter we have considered some conditions that can void the contract absolutely, or where one of the parties can choose to void it if the conditions for voidability are met.

Understanding the classification of contracts into void, voidable, and unenforceable is vital for determining enforceability and rights of the parties. Legal practitioners and laypersons must assess contract terms and the context in which they are entered to identify potential issues early and avoid disputes.

Chapter 7: Quasi Contracts

In this chapter, we discuss the concept of quasi contracts as defined in the Indian Contract Act. Quasi contracts are not contracts in the traditional sense, but obligations imposed by law to prevent unjust enrichment of one party at the expense of another. They are based on the principles of equity, justice, and good conscience.

7.1 Introduction to Quasi-Contracts

A quasi contract is a legal obligation created by the court, in absence of any agreement between the parties. Though there is no contract as such, the law treats the situation as if there were a contract.

Quasi-Contracts are not pure contracts, since they lack all the elements such as offer and acceptance that make up a contract. However, these are relations that resemble some elements of a contract and constitute some form of obligation on the parties similar to a contract.

The Indian contract Act Chapter 5 covers quasi-contracts. These are obligations from one party to another even though they have not entered into a formal contract. These can constitute when a benefit has been received by one party at the expense of another party, and the benefit received is unjust.

The types of quasi contractual relations mentioned in the Indian Contract Act include the following:

- Necessities received by a party who is not eligible or incapable of getting into a contract, such as a lunatic or minor person. An example can be some life-saving medicines or other necessities received by a severely ill or disabled person, who is obliged to pay for them.

- Reimbursement of an amount of money, or arrears, paid by one party to another.
- Enjoyment of some goods of services that are not done gratuitously as a gift. Such gifts have to be paid for by the party that enjoys it.
- Where a party has dropped or misplaced some goods and they have been found by another party, who has the responsibility to return them to the rightful owner.
- Liability by a person to whom money is paid by a party by mistake or coercion. An example can be a bank transfer done by mistake to a wrong account.

7.2 Legal Basis – Sections 68 to 72 of the Indian Contract Act

- **Section 68** – Claim for necessaries supplied to a person incapable of contracting
- **Section 69** – Reimbursement of person paying money due by another, in payment of which he is interested
- **Section 70** – Obligation of person enjoying benefit of a non-gratuitous act
- **Section 71** – Responsibility of finder of goods
- **Section 72** – Liability of person to whom money is paid or thing delivered by mistake or under coercion

7.3 Essential Elements

- There is no formal agreement between parties
- One party is unjustly enriched
- The enrichment is at the expense of the other party
- The enrichment is unjust and inequitable

7.4 Examples of Quasi Contracts

- A supplies food and medicine to B, who is a minor. A is entitled to reimbursement.
- X pays a tax on behalf of Y, in which X has an interest. X can recover the amount.
- A mistakenly transfers money to B's account. B is obligated to return the amount.

7.5 Judicial Interpretations

- *State of West Bengal v. B.K. Mondal and Sons* (1962): The government was held liable to pay for benefits received from construction work, even without a formal contract.
- *Mahabir Kishore v. State of Madhya Pradesh* (1989): Supreme Court held that money paid under mistake of law may be recovered.

7.6 Distinction Between Quasi Contracts and Contracts

Basis	Contract	Quasi Contract
Agreement	Arises from mutual consent	Imposed by law
Intent	Parties intend to create obligation	No such intention exists
Nature	Legal obligation from agreement	Legal obligation from law

7.7 Importance in Modern Context

Quasi contractual obligations are increasingly relevant in digital payments, mistaken transfers, online transactions, and other situations where rapid financial exchanges occur without formal agreements. Courts continue to apply equitable principles to ensure that no party gains unfairly.

7.8 Conclusion

Quasi contracts serve an important role in ensuring fairness where formal agreements are absent. They reinforce the ethical foundation of contract law by obligating parties to restore unjust benefits obtained from others.

Chapter 8: Warranty

In this chapter we discuss the concept of warranty as a contract or part of a contract.

8.1 Introduction to Warranty

Warranty is a type of contract, or one or more conditions present in a contract. A warranty is a promise or guarantee made by a seller concerning the quality or performance of goods offered for sale. It is usually valid for a limited time period. A warranty is a statement of what the seller will do to fix any defect in the product, or if it does not perform as advertised, within the time period of its validity. If the seller does not honor the warranty, the contract is said to be breached.

The sale of goods act 1930 states the following:

13. When condition to be treated as warranty.—

(1) Where a contract of sale is subject to any condition to be fulfilled by the seller, the buyer may waive the condition or elect to treat the breach of the condition as a breach of warranty and not as a ground for treating the contract as repudiated.

(2) Where a contract of sale is not severable and the buyer has accepted the goods or part thereof, the breach of any condition to be fulfilled by the seller can only be treated as a breach of warranty and not as a ground for rejecting the goods and treating the contract as repudiated, unless there is a term of the contract, express or implied, to that effect.

(3) Nothing in this section shall affect the case of any condition or warranty fulfilment of which is excused by law by reason of impossibility or otherwise.

8.2 Types of warranties

There are two types of warranties: express and implied.

- **Express Warranties**: These are explicitly stated promises made by the seller regarding the quality, performance, or durability of the goods or services. For example, a seller stating that a car will give a mileage of 20 km/litre.
- **Implied Warranties**: These are not written or spoken but are imposed by law. Common examples include:
  - **Warranty of quiet possession**: The buyer shall have and enjoy quiet possession of the goods.
  - **Warranty of freedom from encumbrances**: The goods shall be free from any charge or encumbrance.
  - **Warranty as to quality or fitness**: If the buyer makes known the purpose for purchasing the goods, and relies on the seller's expertise, an implied warranty arises that the goods shall be fit for that purpose.

8.3 Difference Between Condition and Warranty

Basis	Condition	Warranty
Importance	Essential to the main purpose of the contract	Collateral to the main purpose
Breach	Leads to repudiation of contract	Only gives rise to a claim for damages
Example	The goods delivered must match the description	Packaging may be defective but usable

8.4 Remedies for Breach of Warranty

- **Damages**: The buyer can claim compensation for loss suffered.
- **No repudiation**: Unlike breach of condition, the buyer cannot reject the goods.

- **Repair or replacement**: Depending on the contract terms, the seller may repair or replace defective goods.

8.5 Warranties in E-Commerce and Consumer Contracts

With the rise of online marketplaces and e-commerce platforms, warranties have become a key part of consumer rights. Many websites offer:

- **Standard warranties** from manufacturers
- **Extended warranties** for an additional fee
- **Return and replacement policies** backed by implied warranties under consumer protection laws

The **Consumer Protection Act, 2019** in India enhances protection for buyers in case of defective products or misleading advertisements, especially in digital transactions.

8.6 Judicial Interpretations

- *Baldry v. Marshall* (1925): Held that a buyer who relies on the seller's skill for a specific purpose may hold the seller liable under an implied warranty.
- *State of Haryana v. S.M. Industrial Corporation* (1995): The court discussed manufacturer warranties and consumer expectations.

8.7 Conclusion

Warranties, whether express or implied, form an important part of consumer and commercial contracts. Understanding them enables buyers to assert their rights and seek remedies when expectations are not met. Legal developments and case law continue to expand the scope and enforceability of warranties in India.

In the following chapter, we look at another law in India related to contracts for sale of goods.

Chapter 9: Sale of Goods Act 1930

In this chapter we discuss the Sale of Goods Act, that defines the law in India related to the sale of goods, such as the rules that should be followed when making a sale. It is another law that was introduced in British India and reflects the similar law in Britain of the time.

9.1 Introduction to the Sale of Goods Act 1930

Sale of Goods Act of 1930 defines the law related to the sale of goods and transfer of ownership, including moveable property but not land.

It mainly focuses on contracts between the buyers and sellers.

THE SALE OF GOODS ACT, 1930

ACT NO. 3 OF 1930[1]

[15th March, 1930.]

An Act to define and amend the law relating to the sale of goods.

WHEREAS it is expedient to define and amend the law relating to the sale of goods; It is hereby enacted as follows:—

CHAPTER I

PRELIMINARY

1. Short title, extent and commencement.—(1) This Act may be called the [2]*** Sale of Goods Act, 1930.

[3][(2) It extends to the whole of India [4][except the State of Jammu and Kashmir].]

(3) It shall come into force on the 1st day of July, 1930.

2. Definitions.—In this Act, unless there is anything repugnant in the subject or context,—

(1) "buyer" means a person who buys or agrees to buy goods;

(2) "delivery" means voluntary transfer of possession from one person to another;

(3) goods are said to be in a "deliverable state" when they are in such state that the buyer would under the contract be bound to take delivery of them;

(4) "document of title to goods" includes a bill of lading, dockwarrant, warehouse keeper's certificate, wharfingers' certificate, railway receipt, [5][multimodal transport document,] warrant or order for the delivery of goods and any other document used in the ordinary course of business as proof of the possession or control of goods, or authorising or purporting to authorise, either by endorsement or by delivery, the possessor of the document to transfer or receive goods thereby

Figure: First page of the Sale of Goods Act 1930

9.2 Contract under sale of goods act

The Sale of Goods Act 1930 defines a contract for a sale of goods between a buyer and a seller, where the ownership of an item is transferred from the seller to the buyer upon payment of a price.

The term goods refers to *"every kind of movable property other than actionable claims and money; and includes stock and shares, growing crops, grass, and things attached to or forming part of the land which are agreed to be severed before sale or under the contract of sale."*

9.3 Transfer of risks and liabilities

Along with the ownership and rights, any risks and liabilities associated with the item are also transferred from the seller to the buyer. The Act covers existing goods as well as goods to be transferred in the future.

The Sale of Goods Act defines what is a contract of sale and the various conditions associated with the contract. It also covers various cases where the goods are faulty or the contract conditions are not met. It covers the rights of the buyers and the sellers, as well as special conditions like damaged goods and auctions.

9.4 Implied Conditions and Warranties in Sale of Goods

The Sale of Goods Act, 1930 provides certain implied conditions and warranties that apply to a contract of sale unless the circumstances of the contract show a different intention. These include:

- **Condition as to title**: The seller has the right to sell the goods.
- **Condition as to description**: Goods must match the description given by the seller.
- **Condition as to quality or fitness**: If the buyer makes known the particular purpose, goods must be fit for that purpose.
- **Condition as to merchantable quality**: Goods must be of a standard that a reasonable person would regard as acceptable.

- **Warranty of quiet possession**: Buyer has the right to enjoy the goods without interference.

9.5 Transfer of Property and Risk

- **Property in goods**: Transfer of ownership from seller to buyer.
- **Risk follows ownership**: Unless otherwise agreed, the risk passes with the property.

The timing of transfer of ownership is crucial for determining liability in case of damage or loss. For specific goods, ownership transfers when the contract is made, unless a contrary intention appears.

9.6 Rights of an Unpaid Seller

An unpaid seller has the following rights:

- **Right of lien**: To retain possession until payment.
- **Right of stoppage in transit**: To stop goods in transit if the buyer becomes insolvent.
- **Right of resale**: To resell goods under certain conditions.
- **Right to sue for price**: If the property has passed to the buyer.

9.7 Remedies for Breach of Contract

- **By Seller**: Damages for non-acceptance, resale, suit for price.
- **By Buyer**: Damages for non-delivery, specific performance, refund of price.

9.8 Relevance in Modern Commerce

In the age of e-commerce and digital trade, the Sale of Goods Act continues to apply to both online and offline sales. Online sellers and platforms are bound by the same principles of transfer of ownership, fitness of goods, and consumer protection.

Courts have increasingly applied the Act to cases involving:

- Non-delivery or defective delivery in online shopping
- Misrepresentation of goods on digital platforms
- Delay or breach in high-volume B2B supply contracts

9.9 Case Law Highlights

- *Bharat Petroleum Corp. Ltd. v. Great Eastern Shipping Co. Ltd.* (2008): Clarified the passing of property and applicability of risk.
- *Kailash Nath Associates v. DDA* (2015): Reiterated the importance of readiness and willingness in performance.
- *National Seeds Corp. Ltd. v. M. Madhusudhan Reddy* (2012): The seller was held liable under implied warranty for defective seeds.

9.10 Conclusion

The Sale of Goods Act, 1930 plays a pivotal role in regulating commercial transactions. Its provisions continue to remain relevant in governing the duties, rights, and liabilities of both buyers and sellers in the changing landscape of trade and consumer protection.

Chapter 10: Breach of Contract and Remedies

In this chapter, we discuss what happens when a party fails to perform their part of the contract. This failure is known as a breach of contract. We also examine the legal remedies available to the aggrieved party under Indian law, along with examples and practical steps.

10.1 What is Breach of Contract?

A breach of contract occurs when one of the parties fails to perform their obligations under the contract. It may happen in the following ways:

Actual breach: When a party refuses or fails to perform their contractual obligation on the due date or during the performance period.

Anticipatory breach: When one party declares in advance, either by words or conduct, that they will not fulfill their part of the contract when due.

A breach can be total or partial. A total breach renders the entire contract unenforceable, while a partial breach may relate to only some terms or conditions.

10.2 Legal Remedies for Breach of Contract

The Indian Contract Act, 1872, outlines several remedies for breach of contract. These remedies aim to compensate the aggrieved party and, in some cases, ensure performance.

Damages: Monetary compensation is the most common remedy. There are different types:

Ordinary damages: These are direct losses arising naturally from the breach.

Special damages: These are additional losses that were foreseeable and communicated to the breaching party at the time of the contract.

Nominal damages: Small amounts awarded where a legal right is violated but no substantial loss is proved.

Exemplary or punitive damages: Rare in contract law, awarded in exceptional cases involving wrongful conduct beyond mere breach.

Specific Performance: In cases where damages are not adequate—such as contracts involving unique goods or property—the court may order the party to perform their contractual duties. This is a discretionary remedy and subject to limitations.

Injunction: A court may restrain a party from breaching the contract or doing any act contrary to it. Injunctions are often used in cases involving non-compete or non-disclosure agreements.

Rescission: The contract is cancelled, and both parties are restored to their original position. This is often used when the contract was formed based on misrepresentation or undue influence.

Quantum Meruit: This Latin term means "as much as is deserved." It allows a party to claim payment for the portion of work completed when the contract is partially performed.

10.3 How to File a Claim for Breach

When a breach occurs, the aggrieved party should take the following steps:

Document the breach: Keep a record of all communications, invoices, or proofs of non-performance.

Send a legal notice: Inform the breaching party in writing about the breach and demand remedy or performance.

Attempt resolution: Parties may attempt to settle the dispute through negotiation or mediation.

File a lawsuit: If resolution fails, a civil suit may be filed in a competent court. The limitation period for filing such a suit is typically three years from the date of breach.

Court process: The court may conduct hearings and issue orders based on evidence and applicable laws.

10.4 Case Example

In Hadley v. Baxendale (1854), a landmark English case, the court ruled that damages for breach must be such as may fairly and reasonably be considered either arising naturally or such as may reasonably be supposed to have been in the contemplation of both parties at the time of contract.

In India, similar principles apply. In Karsandas H. Thacker v. Saran Engineering Co. (AIR 1965 SC 1981), the Supreme Court held that loss of expected profits cannot be claimed as damages unless it was in the contemplation of both parties at the time the contract was made.

10.5 Practical Example

Suppose A agrees to deliver 100 chairs to B for an event. A fails to deliver on time, causing B to rent other chairs at a higher cost. B can sue A for the extra expense incurred due to the breach, as well as other consequential losses.

10.6 Conclusion

Breach of contract is a common legal issue that affects individuals and businesses alike. The Indian Contract Act provides a comprehensive framework of remedies to address such breaches. Understanding these remedies helps in asserting one's legal rights and pursuing appropriate action when contracts are not honored.

Chapter 11: E-Contracts and Digital Signatures

In this chapter, we explore how modern technology has influenced contract law, especially through the rise of electronic contracts (e-contracts) and digital signatures. These developments have gained recognition under Indian law and are now a key part of business transactions and daily life, especially with the rise of digital banking, e-commerce, and remote work.

11.1 Introduction to E-Contracts

An e-contract is a legally binding contract created and executed in an electronic format. It includes contracts made via email, click-wrap agreements on websites, mobile app-based consent forms, and even agreements over instant messaging apps. Under Indian law, e-contracts are legally valid and enforceable, subject to certain conditions.

The Information Technology Act, 2000 provides the legal framework for recognizing electronic contracts in India. Section 10A of the IT Act validates contracts formed through electronic means and removes doubts about enforceability merely due to their digital form.

11.2 Types of E-Contracts

E-contracts generally fall into three types:

- **Click-wrap agreements**: Contracts where users click an "I Agree" button to accept terms (e.g., software installs, website terms).
- **Browse-wrap agreements**: Terms available through a hyperlink, where usage of a website implies consent. These are

more controversial legally and depend on notice and access.

- **Email contracts**: Formal agreements exchanged and confirmed over email or electronic messaging platforms. If offer and acceptance can be proved, the contract is valid.

11.3 Legal Validity of E-Contracts in India

E-contracts are considered valid under Indian law if they fulfil the essential elements of a contract as stated in the Indian Contract Act:

- Lawful offer and acceptance
- Consideration
- Capacity to contract
- Free consent
- Lawful object

In addition, the IT Act requires that electronic records and digital signatures be reliable and secure. For example, acceptance of terms must be clear, informed, and traceable.

11.4 Digital Signatures

A digital signature is a secure electronic signature that uses cryptographic algorithms to verify the identity of the sender and the integrity of the document. It is not merely an image of a signature, but a coded confirmation issued by a Certifying Authority (CA).

In India, digital signatures are regulated under the IT Act and must be issued by a licensed Certifying Authority, such as eMudhra or Sify. The law requires:

- Use of asymmetric encryption
- Attachment of digital certificate to validate identity
- Secure key management

Section 3 of the IT Act lays down the criteria for a valid digital signature. Digital signatures ensure:

- **Authentication** of the sender
- **Integrity** of the message
- **Non-repudiation**, meaning the sender cannot later deny sending the message

11.5 Electronic Authentication Techniques

Besides digital signatures, the IT Act and associated frameworks permit other methods of electronic authentication such as:

- **Aadhaar-based eKYC authentication**: Often used for opening bank accounts, mutual fund investments, and telecom services.
- **OTP (One Time Password)** based verification: Used for signing documents, confirming purchases, or accessing portals.
- **Biometric authentication**: Thumbprint or iris scan verification is increasingly used in government schemes and secure applications.

These methods provide flexibility, but for critical documents, only digital signatures offer strong legal enforceability.

11.6 Limitations and Exceptions

Not all types of contracts can be executed electronically. According to Section 1(4) of the IT Act, the following are excluded from electronic contracting:

- Wills and testamentary dispositions
- Negotiable instruments (except cheques)

- Trust deeds
- Power of attorney documents
- Contracts for sale or transfer of immovable property

These documents still require traditional ink signatures and physical stamping to be valid.

11.7 Sectoral Uses of E-Contracts in India

E-contracts are widely used in various sectors:

- **E-commerce**: Terms and conditions agreed while shopping online.
- **Banking and Finance**: Loan applications, credit card consents, KYC updates.
- **Employment**: Offer letters, NDAs, and remote work agreements.
- **Education**: Admission agreements and online course terms.
- **Healthcare**: Patient consent forms for teleconsultations.

Startups and digital-first companies often rely heavily on e-contracts to reduce paperwork and speed up operations.

11.8 Practical Example

Suppose a freelance graphic designer agrees to create a logo for a client. The agreement is made over email, where the terms, price, and timeline are all clearly discussed and confirmed. This email exchange forms a legally valid e-contract if all elements of a contract are present.

In another example, when a user signs up for an online streaming service and accepts the terms and conditions by clicking a checkbox, it constitutes a valid click-wrap agreement. If a dispute arises over cancellation fees or content restrictions, the company can point to the user's digital acceptance of the terms.

11.9 Conclusion

E-contracts and digital signatures have transformed the way contracts are formed and executed in India. They offer convenience, traceability, and scalability—especially important in the digital economy. However, they must be entered into with the same caution and understanding as traditional contracts. As technology evolves, legal frameworks will continue to adapt to support secure, enforceable, and transparent digital agreements.

Chapter 12: Standard Form Contracts and Consumer Protection

In this chapter, we examine standard form contracts—commonly known as boilerplate contracts—which are pre-drafted agreements used in mass transactions. These contracts are frequently encountered in sectors such as insurance, banking, telecommunications, e-commerce, and real estate. We also explore how Indian law, including the Consumer Protection Act, addresses the power imbalance between parties and provides remedies against unfair contract terms.

12.1 What is a Standard Form Contract?

A standard form contract is a pre-prepared contract where most terms are set in advance by one party (usually the seller or service provider) and the other party (typically the consumer) has little or no ability to negotiate or modify the terms.

These are often offered on a "take it or leave it" basis. For example, when a customer signs up for a mobile phone connection or an insurance policy, the terms are usually fixed by the service provider.

12.2 Key Features of Standard Form Contracts

- **Lack of negotiation**: The consumer cannot alter the terms.
- **Repetition and volume**: Used in numerous identical transactions.
- **One-sided obligations**: The drafting party enjoys legal or practical advantages.
- **Fine print**: Important terms are often buried in lengthy clauses or legal jargon.

12.3 Common Examples in India

- Insurance policies
- Railway or airline tickets
- Terms of service on websites and apps
- Banking forms for loans, credit cards
- Apartment builder-buyer agreements

12.4 Legal Concerns with Standard Form Contracts

Due to their one-sided nature, these contracts can be unfair or exploitative. Common problematic clauses include:

- Unilateral right to modify terms without consent
- Exclusion of liability for negligence
- Restrictions on legal recourse or jurisdiction
- Excessive penalties or forfeiture clauses

Indian courts have held that just because a party signed a standard contract does not mean all terms are automatically valid. Courts may strike down terms that are:

- Unconscionable
- Contrary to public policy
- In violation of fundamental rights

12.5 Judicial Oversight and Case Law

In *Central Inland Water Transport Corporation Ltd. v. Brojo Nath Ganguly* (1986 AIR 1571), the Supreme Court invalidated an unfair termination clause in a standard employment contract as being against public policy.

In *LIC of India v. Consumer Education and Research Centre* (1995 AIR 1811), the court emphasized that standard form contracts must pass the test of fairness and reasonableness.

12.6 The Role of Consumer Protection Act, 2019

The Consumer Protection Act, 2019 provides remedies against unfair trade practices, defective goods, and deficient services. It explicitly empowers consumer forums to:

- Declare terms of a contract to be **unfair**
- Order **modification** of such contracts
- Provide **compensation** for unfair conduct or loss

The Act defines an **unfair contract** as one which:

- Causes a significant change in consumer rights
- Imposes unreasonable conditions or obligations
- Results in unjust benefit to the service provider

12.7 Safeguards for Consumers

Consumers should take the following precautions:

- Read the contract carefully before signing
- Ask for clarifications on confusing clauses
- Check refund and cancellation policies
- Be aware of arbitration or jurisdiction clauses
- Approach consumer forums for redressal if mistreated

12.8 Government and Regulatory Measures

Regulators such as SEBI, RBI, IRDAI, and TRAI have issued guidelines for transparency in contracts related to financial services, insurance, and telecom services. These include mandates for:

- Standardization of product disclosures
- Highlighting key clauses
- Plain language summaries

12.9 Practical Example

Suppose a consumer signs up for a home loan and later discovers that the bank has increased the interest rate without notice. If the clause enabling this was buried in fine print and not explained clearly, it could be considered an unfair term. The consumer can seek remedy from a consumer court.

12.10 Conclusion

Standard form contracts are convenient but can lead to abuse of power if not regulated. Indian courts and consumer protection laws have evolved to safeguard the rights of consumers by subjecting such contracts to fairness tests. As consumers, understanding one's rights and being vigilant before signing any contract is key to preventing exploitation.

Chapter 13: Employment Agreements and Contract Law

In this chapter, we explore employment agreements, which are a specific type of contract between an employer and an employee. These agreements form the legal foundation of the employer-employee relationship, outlining the rights, responsibilities, compensation, and terms of service. We examine how Indian contract law applies to employment contracts, what clauses are commonly included, and the limits of enforceability, particularly in the context of labour rights and judicial scrutiny.

13.1 Nature of Employment Agreements

An employment agreement is a contract between an employer and employee that governs the terms of employment. It may be written, verbal, or implied through conduct, but a written contract offers the greatest clarity and legal protection.

As per Section 10 of the Indian Contract Act, 1872, employment contracts must meet the criteria for a valid contract: offer, acceptance, consideration, legal capacity, free consent, and lawful object.

13.2 Common Terms in Employment Contracts

Typical clauses in employment agreements include:

- Job role and responsibilities
- Working hours and location
- Remuneration, bonuses, and benefits
- Probation period and confirmation
- Leave entitlements

- Termination clauses
- Confidentiality and non-disclosure
- Non-compete and non-solicitation
- Dispute resolution

13.3 Probation, Notice Periods, and Termination

During the probation period, which typically ranges from 3 to 6 months, employment may be terminated with shorter notice. Post-confirmation, the notice period is usually one to three months.

Termination clauses must be fair and not arbitrary. Courts have invalidated clauses that give employers unilateral rights to terminate without cause or notice. Employers are also bound by the provisions of the Industrial Disputes Act, 1947, in case of retrenchment.

13.4 Enforceability of Restrictive Clauses

Employment contracts often include clauses to restrict the employee's actions even after employment ends:

- **Non-compete clauses**: Restrict employees from working for a competitor after resignation.
- **Non-solicitation clauses**: Prevent employees from poaching clients or co-workers.

Indian courts, however, have generally held that post-employment non-compete clauses are void under Section 27 of the Indian Contract Act, unless they are reasonable and limited in scope, duration, and geography.

13.5 Bonds and Training Reimbursement Agreements

Companies sometimes require employees to sign bonds agreeing to serve for a fixed duration or repay training costs if they resign early. Courts have upheld such clauses if:

- The training was substantial and valuable.
- The bond period is reasonable.
- The compensation is not in the nature of penalty.

However, excessive penalties or coercion may render the bond unenforceable.

13.6 Employment Law vs Contract Law

While contract law governs the formation and terms of the employment agreement, labour laws provide statutory protection to workers. Some of the relevant labour laws include:

- Industrial Disputes Act, 1947
- Shops and Establishments Acts (state-wise)
- Payment of Wages Act, 1936
- Minimum Wages Act, 1948
- Employees' Provident Funds and Miscellaneous Provisions Act, 1952

These laws override any contractual terms that provide less favourable treatment than what is guaranteed by statute.

13.7 Judicial Oversight and Case Law

In *Superintendence Company of India v. Sh. Krishan Murgai* (1980 AIR 1717), the Supreme Court held that a post-employment restraint clause preventing an employee from joining a rival business was unenforceable under Section 27 of the Contract Act.

In *Neha Bhadwaj v. Infosys Technologies Ltd.* (2008), a Delhi court upheld a training bond that required reimbursement of costs if the employee left before one year.

13.8 Practical Example

Suppose an IT company hires a software developer and signs a contract that includes a one-year service bond with a ₹1 lakh penalty for early resignation. If the employee resigns after six months, the company may recover a proportionate amount, provided the bond is not excessive and the training was meaningful.

However, if the company includes a clause that says the employee cannot work in any other IT firm for two years, such a clause is likely to be struck down as unreasonable and void under Indian contract law.

13.9 Conclusion

Employment agreements are vital tools for defining the terms of work and safeguarding the rights of both employers and employees. While contract law provides the framework for enforceability, it is essential that these contracts align with labour laws and do not contain unfair or unreasonable clauses. Understanding the legal limits of employment contracts helps prevent exploitation and ensures a balanced work relationship.

Chapter 14: Government Contracts and Tenders

Government contracts are a significant area of contract law in India. They involve agreements where one of the parties is a government body or public sector undertaking (PSU). These contracts are subject not only to general principles of the Indian Contract Act, 1872, but also to constitutional provisions and administrative law principles. In this chapter, we explore the unique features, rules, and legal safeguards associated with government contracts.

14.1 What are Government Contracts?

A government contract is an agreement entered into by the government (Central, State, or local bodies) with a private party, individual, or firm for procuring goods, services, or executing public works. These contracts are governed by Article 298 of the Indian Constitution, which gives the Union and the States the power to contract.

14.2 Legal Framework Governing Government Contracts

Apart from the Indian Contract Act, the following laws and guidelines apply:

- **Article 299 of the Constitution of India**: Specifies that all contracts made by the Union or a State must be expressed in the name of the President or Governor and must be executed by authorized persons.
- **General Financial Rules (GFR), 2017**: Prescribe procedures for public procurement and tendering.

- **Manuals and Procurement Guidelines**: Issued by departments like the Ministry of Finance, CPWD, or PSUs.

Non-compliance with Article 299 may render a contract void and unenforceable.

14.3 Tendering Process and Types of Tenders

Government contracts are usually awarded through a formal tendering process to ensure transparency and fair competition. Common types include:

- **Open Tender**: Public invitation to all eligible bidders.
- **Limited Tender**: Sent to a limited number of empanelled vendors.
- **Single Tender**: Used in emergency or when only one vendor is available.
- **E-Tendering**: Online portal-based bidding (e.g., GEM – Government e-Marketplace).

The tender document usually includes eligibility criteria, scope of work, bid validity, price bid format, and contract terms.

14.4 Essential Clauses in Government Contracts

- Scope of work and specifications
- Delivery timelines and milestones
- Payment terms
- Liquidated damages for delay
- Termination and force majeure
- Dispute resolution mechanism (often arbitration)
- Performance guarantee and security deposit

14.5 Challenges and Legal Disputes

Disputes may arise from:

- Non-performance or delays
- Rejection of bids
- Blacklisting or debarment
- Breach of tender terms

Contractors may approach High Courts under Article 226 if administrative actions are arbitrary or violate principles of natural justice.

14.6 Judicial Viewpoint

In *R.D. Shetty v. International Airport Authority of India* (AIR 1979 SC 1628), the Supreme Court held that even contractual matters involving the state must comply with Article 14 and be fair and non-arbitrary.

In *Tata Cellular v. Union of India* (AIR 1996 SC 11), the Court observed that judicial review is limited to the decision-making process in government tenders, not the merits of the decision.

14.7 Blacklisting and Its Consequences

Government bodies may blacklist firms for default, fraud, or misconduct. However, the procedure must be fair and include an opportunity to be heard. Courts have ruled that blacklisting without notice violates principles of natural justice.

14.8 Practical Example

Suppose a construction firm wins a government tender to build a bridge but fails to complete the project on time. The government may invoke the liquidated damages clause and deduct penalties. If the firm disputes this, the matter may go to arbitration, and courts may intervene only on limited grounds.

14.9 Conclusion

Government contracts are complex and regulated by both contract law and administrative law. The principles of fairness, transparency, and accountability play a critical role. Understanding the constitutional and procedural safeguards is essential for any party entering into agreements with government entities.

Chapter 15: Force Majeure and Frustration of Contract

In this chapter, we explore the doctrines of force majeure and frustration of contract. These legal principles deal with situations where unforeseen events prevent parties from fulfilling their contractual obligations. Understanding these doctrines is essential in times of crises such as natural disasters, pandemics, or political upheavals, where contractual performance becomes impossible or impractical.

15.1 What is Force Majeure?

Force majeure refers to unforeseeable and uncontrollable events that prevent a party from performing their obligations under a contract. These may include natural disasters (earthquakes, floods), war, terrorism, strikes, pandemics, or government-imposed lockdowns.

A force majeure clause is typically included in contracts to excuse or delay performance without penalty during such events. However, for it to be enforceable, it must be expressly written into the contract and clearly define the triggering events.

15.2 Legal Basis and Interpretation in India

In Indian law, force majeure is governed by Section 32 of the Indian Contract Act, 1872, which deals with contingent contracts—those dependent on the occurrence or non-occurrence of a future uncertain event.

The courts have held that force majeure must not only be unforeseen but must also directly prevent contractual performance. Mere difficulty or increased cost does not qualify.

15.3 Frustration of Contract

When no force majeure clause exists, or when the event is not covered, parties may rely on the doctrine of frustration under Section 56 of the Indian Contract Act. This section states:

- An agreement to do an act impossible in itself is void.
- A contract becomes void if, after its formation, it becomes impossible to perform due to an event beyond the control of the parties.

Frustration automatically discharges both parties from further obligations, and neither party can claim damages.

15.4 Key Conditions for Frustration

- The event must occur after the contract was formed.
- The event must render the performance impossible or unlawful.
- The event must not have been caused by either party.
- The contract must not already have provided for the event in question.

15.5 Differences Between Force Majeure and Frustration

Aspect	Force Majeure	Frustration of Contract
Based on Clause	Requires specific clause in contract	No clause needed; statutory provision
Result	May suspend, delay, or terminate contract	Automatically renders contract void
Governing Section	Section 32	Section 56
Damages	Depends on clause terms	No damages can be claimed

15.6 Judicial Interpretation

In *Energy Watchdog v. CERC* (2017), the Supreme Court ruled that force majeure clauses must be strictly interpreted and cannot be expanded by analogy.

In *Satyabrata Ghose v. Mugneeram Bangur & Co.* (AIR 1954 SC 44), the Court explained that frustration applies only where the fundamental basis of the contract is destroyed.

During the COVID-19 pandemic, several High Courts ruled that lockdowns could constitute force majeure depending on the wording of the contract.

15.7 Practical Example

Suppose a company contracts to supply machinery from a foreign manufacturer. A sudden war disrupts all shipping routes. If the contract includes a force majeure clause covering war, the delay or non-performance may be excused. If no such clause exists, the supplier may claim frustration under Section 56.

However, if the delay is due to rising prices or worker shortages, neither force majeure nor frustration may apply, as these are commercial risks.

15.8 Drafting Effective Force Majeure Clauses

- List specific events (e.g., natural disasters, acts of God, war, epidemics).
- Clarify obligations during suspension (e.g., notice, mitigation).
- Define the duration after which termination may occur.
- Specify exclusions (e.g., financial hardship or negligence).

15.9 Conclusion

The doctrines of force majeure and frustration provide relief in genuine cases of impossibility but must be applied cautiously. Contracts should be carefully drafted with clear force majeure provisions to avoid ambiguity and reduce the need for litigation. Understanding these legal tools is vital for risk management, especially in uncertain times.

Chapter 16: International Contracts and Cross-Border Enforcement

In today's globalized world, contracts often involve parties from different countries. International contracts are commercial agreements where at least one party is based outside India or where performance spans across borders. In this chapter, we examine the nature, challenges, and legal frameworks for enforcing international contracts under Indian law and global conventions.

16.1 Nature of International Contracts

International contracts include agreements such as:

- Import-export contracts
- Cross-border service contracts
- Technology licensing and IP transfer agreements
- Joint ventures or foreign collaborations
- International sales of goods and franchising

These contracts typically involve multiple legal systems and currencies, and require careful drafting to address jurisdiction, governing law, dispute resolution, and enforcement.

16.2 Choice of Law and Jurisdiction

Parties to an international contract can agree on:

- **Governing law**: Which country's laws will apply to the interpretation of the contract
- **Jurisdiction**: Which court or legal forum will hear disputes

Indian courts generally respect these clauses if freely agreed by the parties. However, they will not enforce foreign laws that violate Indian public policy or statutory rights.

16.3 International Legal Instruments

Several international conventions guide cross-border contracting:

- **United Nations Convention on Contracts for the International Sale of Goods (CISG)**: Applies to the sale of goods between parties in different countries (India is not a signatory).
- **Hague Principles on Choice of Law in International Contracts**: Promote freedom of choice in determining applicable law.
- **New York Convention, 1958**: Facilitates recognition and enforcement of foreign arbitral awards in member countries, including India.

16.4 Enforcement of Foreign Judgments in India

Foreign judgments may be enforced in Indian courts under:

- **Section 13 and 14 of the Code of Civil Procedure, 1908 (CPC)**
- **Reciprocity Agreements**: Judgments from "reciprocating territories" can be directly enforced as a decree (e.g., UK, Singapore).

The Indian court will ensure:

- The judgment is by a court of competent jurisdiction
- The judgment is not contrary to natural justice or Indian public policy

- The judgment is final and conclusive

16.5 Enforcement of Foreign Arbitral Awards

India is a signatory to the **New York Convention** and the **Geneva Convention**. The Arbitration and Conciliation Act, 1996 (Part II) governs the enforcement of foreign awards in India.

Indian courts may refuse enforcement only if:

- Parties were under incapacity
- Award deals with non-arbitrable subject matter
- The award is against Indian public policy

16.6 Dispute Resolution Mechanisms

International contracts often include arbitration clauses. Popular arbitration centers include:

- Singapore International Arbitration Centre (SIAC)
- London Court of International Arbitration (LCIA)
- International Chamber of Commerce (ICC)
- Indian Council of Arbitration (ICA)

Mediation and conciliation are also used to resolve cross-border disputes amicably.

16.7 Currency and Payment Terms

Contracts must clearly specify:

- Currency of payment
- Exchange rate mechanism
- Payment timelines and applicable taxes

The Foreign Exchange Management Act (FEMA), 1999 governs cross-border remittances and compliance in India.

16.8 Practical Example

Suppose an Indian textile exporter signs a contract with a European retailer. The contract specifies English law as governing law and ICC arbitration in Paris. If a dispute arises, the arbitration award can be enforced in India under the New York Convention, provided it complies with procedural fairness and public policy.

Alternatively, if the European retailer fails to pay and the exporter seeks to enforce a UK court judgment in India, the exporter must file execution proceedings in an Indian court under Section 44A of the CPC.

16.9 Challenges in Cross-Border Contracts

- Language and translation issues
- Conflicting legal systems
- Delays in enforcement
- Political risks and regulatory changes
- Difficulty in serving legal notices abroad

16.10 Conclusion

International contracts offer vast opportunities but come with complexities. Proper drafting, awareness of foreign laws, and the inclusion of robust dispute resolution and enforcement clauses are essential. With careful planning, businesses can reduce legal uncertainty and benefit from cross-border collaboration.

Chapter 17: Drafting a Simple Contract

In this chapter, we offer a step-by-step guide to drafting a simple yet legally valid contract. Whether you're forming a service agreement, renting out property, or entering into a freelance deal, understanding how to write a basic contract is an essential skill for individuals and small businesses. This chapter outlines the structure, essential clauses, and drafting tips for a clear, enforceable contract.

17.1 Importance of Good Drafting

A well-drafted contract helps:

- Avoid misunderstandings
- Clarify roles and responsibilities
- Reduce the risk of disputes
- Protect legal rights in case of breach

Even a simple agreement, if written clearly and comprehensively, can prevent expensive litigation.

17.2 Core Elements of a Valid Contract

Every valid contract under Indian law must contain the following:

- **Offer and Acceptance**: Clear proposal and unambiguous acceptance
- **Consideration**: Something of value exchanged
- **Capacity to Contract**: Parties must be legally competent
- **Free Consent**: No coercion, fraud, undue influence, or misrepresentation
- **Lawful Object**: Purpose must be legal and not against public

policy

17.3 Structure of a Simple Contract

A basic contract may be structured into the following sections:

1. **Title**: Name of the agreement (e.g., Freelance Graphic Design Agreement)
2. **Date**: The effective date of the agreement
3. **Parties**: Names, addresses, and legal identity of the contracting parties
4. **Recitals**: Background or purpose of the agreement (optional)
5. **Definitions**: Any key terms used in the agreement
6. **Obligations**: Specific duties and responsibilities of each party
7. **Payment Terms**: Amount, mode, and timeline for payment
8. **Timelines and Deliverables**: Project milestones, if applicable
9. **Termination Clause**: Conditions under which the contract can end
10. **Confidentiality Clause**: Restricts sharing of sensitive information
11. **Governing Law and Jurisdiction**: Indian law and city of dispute resolution
12. **Signatures**: Signatures of both parties with name, date, and place

17.4 Sample Template

Service Agreement

This Agreement is made on this 1st day of July, 2025, between:

A. Ravi Kumar, residing at 123 Park Street, Bangalore ("Client")

AND

B. Priya Singh, Freelance Web Developer, residing at 45 Green Lane, Pune ("Service Provider")

Scope of Work: Priya Singh agrees to design and deliver a 5-page business website for Ravi Kumar by 31 July 2025.

Fees: ₹25,000 to be paid in two installments: ₹10,000 upfront and ₹15,000 upon completion.

Termination: Either party may terminate this agreement with 7 days' notice.

Governing Law: This contract shall be governed by the laws of India and subject to courts in Bangalore.

Signatures:

Ravi Kumar (Client) Priya Singh (Service Provider)

Date: ________ Date: ________

17.5 Tips for Effective Contract Drafting

- Use clear, simple language
- Avoid ambiguity and vague phrases
- Define key terms
- Make sure all obligations are reciprocal and measurable
- Include fallback provisions in case of delays or non-performance
- Always include a dispute resolution method
- Review the contract before signing; consult a legal professional if needed

17.6 Common Mistakes to Avoid

- Relying solely on verbal agreements

- Using generic templates without customization
- Omitting termination or dispute clauses
- Failing to date or sign the document
- Ignoring tax or regulatory implications

17.7 Conclusion

Drafting a simple contract is not difficult if one understands the basic principles and structure. Even a short, clearly written agreement can offer significant legal protection. Individuals and small businesses are encouraged to document their dealings properly and adopt good contracting practices to minimize risks and ensure professional conduct.

Chapter 18: Contract Templates for Common Use Cases

In this chapter, we provide sample templates for common types of contracts used in daily life and small businesses. These examples can serve as starting points and should be tailored to specific needs with legal advice where appropriate.

18.1 Freelance Services Agreement

Freelance Services Agreement

This Agreement is made on [Date] between:

Client: [Full Name, Address] **Service Provider**: [Full Name, Address]

Scope of Work: [Describe services to be delivered] **Fees and Payment**: [Amount, payment method, schedule] **Timeline**: [Project deadlines or milestones] **Termination**: Either party may terminate with [X] days' notice. **Confidentiality**: Parties agree to keep confidential information secure. **Dispute Resolution**: Any dispute shall be subject to courts in [City].

18.2 Rental Agreement for Residential Property

Residential Rental Agreement

This Agreement is made on [Date] between:

Landlord: [Full Name, Address]

Tenant: [Full Name, Address]

Property: [Full address of rented property] **Monthly Rent**: ₹[Amount], payable by the 5th of every month. **Security Deposit**: ₹[Amount] **Duration**: [e.g., 11 months] **Utilities and Maintenance**: [Specify responsibilities] **Termination**: [Notice period for vacating]

18.3 Loan Agreement Between Friends or Family

Personal Loan Agreement

This Agreement is made on [Date] between:

Lender: [Full Name, Address]

Borrower: [Full Name, Address]

Loan Amount: ₹[Amount]

Repayment Terms: [e.g., monthly payments, interest if any] **Due Date**: [Final due date] **Optional Clause**: No legal interest shall be charged unless specified in writing.

18.4 Employee Appointment Letter

Appointment Letter

Dear [Employee Name],

We are pleased to offer you the position of [Job Title] at [Company Name], effective from [Start Date].

Salary: ₹[Amount] per month

Work Hours: [e.g., 9 AM – 6 PM, Monday to Friday]

Probation Period: [e.g., 6 months]

Leave: [e.g., 18 days of annual leave] **Termination**: [e.g., 30 days' notice by either party]

Please sign below to accept this offer.

18.5 Memorandum of Understanding (MoU)

Memorandum of Understanding (MoU)

This MoU is made on [Date] between:

Party A: [Name, Organization, Address]

Party B: [Name, Organization, Address]

Purpose: To collaborate on [project/initiative].

This MoU is not legally binding but expresses mutual intentions.

18.6 Conclusion

These templates provide a basic foundation for frequently used contracts. They should be modified to suit specific needs and reviewed by a legal professional for important or high-stakes agreements. Clear and proper documentation helps build trust and reduce disputes in personal and business relationships.

Chapter 19: Conclusion

This book has offered a comprehensive introduction to the principles of contract law as applicable in India. Beginning with the basic definition and history of contracts, we examined essential concepts such as offer and acceptance, free consent, consideration, and the capacity to contract. Further, we explored important legal frameworks like the Indian Contract Act, 1872 and the Sale of Goods Act, 1930, and discussed their relevance in both traditional and modern commercial settings.

We also addressed specific issues including fraud, misrepresentation, and coercion; the distinction between void and voidable contracts; quasi-contracts; warranties; and the implications of vicarious liability. Additional topics such as contracts related to minors, digital transactions, consumer protection, and liability in tort contexts have been woven in to highlight the evolving nature of contractual obligations in contemporary India.

The book concludes with useful contract templates and a glossary, serving as a practical resource for students, professionals, and general readers alike. By understanding the legal principles and real-world implications of contract law, readers will be better equipped to navigate, draft, and analyse agreements with clarity and confidence.

As mentioned, a strong contract law whose terms are enforced is essential for the development of a free market in trade and commerce in any country. The Indian Contract Act serves to fill such a demand in India.

It is hoped that this book will be a valuable guide for anyone seeking to understand, navigate, and apply contract law in India.

Glossary of Legal Terms in Contract Law

This glossary provides definitions of common legal terms encountered in contract law. It is intended to help readers better understand the terminology used in agreements and legal discussions.

Acceptance: Agreement to the terms of an offer, creating a binding contract.

Arbitration: A method of resolving disputes outside of courts, where a neutral third party makes a binding decision.

Breach of Contract: Failure by a party to fulfil their obligations under a contract.

Clause: A specific provision or section within a contract.

Coercion: Forcing a party to enter into a contract through threats or unlawful pressure.

Consideration: Something of value exchanged between parties to form a valid contract.

Contract: A legally enforceable agreement between two or more parties.

Damages: Monetary compensation awarded to an injured party in the event of a contract breach.

Force Majeure: A clause in a contract that frees parties from liability due to extraordinary events beyond their control.

Frustration of Contract: A situation where unforeseen events render a contract impossible to perform, making it void.

Governing Law: The legal system under which a contract will be interpreted and enforced.

Indemnity: A contractual promise to compensate for loss or damage.

Injunction: A court order requiring a party to do or refrain from doing a specific act.

Jurisdiction: The authority of a court or legal body to hear and decide a case.

Misrepresentation: False or misleading statements made to induce a party into a contract.

Offer: A proposal by one party to enter into a contract on certain terms.

Performance: Fulfilment of contractual obligations by a party.

Quasi Contract: Legal obligation imposed by law in the absence of a formal contract to prevent unjust enrichment.

Rescission: Cancellation of a contract and restoration of parties to their original positions.

Specific Performance: A court order requiring a party to perform their obligations under the contract.

Termination: Ending a contract before completion, either by mutual consent or due to breach or other conditions.

Void Contract: A contract that is not legally enforceable from the outset.

Voidable Contract: A contract that is valid until one party chooses to void it due to certain defects like coercion or misrepresentation.

Warranty: A promise in a contract regarding the condition or quality of goods or services.

Agency: A legal relationship in which one party (the agent) is authorised to act on behalf of another (the principal) and thereby create legal relations with third parties.

Bailment: The delivery of goods by one person (the bailor) to another (the bailee) for a specific purpose, on the condition that the goods shall be returned or otherwise dealt with according to the bailor's instructions.

Condition: A fundamental term in a contract that goes to the root of the agreement. Breach of a condition entitles the innocent party to repudiate the contract and claim damages.

Contingent Contract: A contract to do or not to do something if some event, collateral to such contract, does or does not happen (Section 31, Indian Contract Act, 1872).

Discharge of Contract: The termination of contractual obligations, which may occur by performance, agreement, breach, frustration, or operation of law.

Estoppel: A legal principle that prevents a party from asserting a fact or claim that is inconsistent with a position previously taken, especially where that inconsistency would cause harm to another party who reasonably relied on the original position.

Guarantee: A contract by which one person undertakes to discharge the liability of a third person in case of that person's default (Section 126, Indian Contract Act, 1872).

Lien: The right of one party to retain possession of goods belonging to another until a debt owed by that other party is paid.

Liquidated Damages: A sum agreed upon by contracting parties at the time of entering into a contract as the amount of compensation payable in the event of a specified breach.

Minor: A person who has not attained the age of majority (18 years under the Indian Majority Act, 1875, or 21 years if a guardian has been appointed). A minor's agreement is void ab initio under Indian law.

Novation: The substitution of a new contract in place of an existing one, either by changing the parties or the terms, with the consent of all parties involved.

Pledge: The bailment of goods as security for payment of a debt or performance of a promise (Section 172, Indian Contract Act, 1872).

Privity of Contract: The principle that only the parties to a contract can sue or be sued on it. A third party generally cannot enforce rights under a contract to which it is not a party.

Promissory Estoppel: A legal doctrine that prevents a party from going back on a promise, even without formal consideration, if the other party has relied on that promise to their detriment.

Restitution: The restoration of a benefit conferred on a party under a contract that has been declared void or rescinded, so as to prevent unjust enrichment.

Undue Influence: The improper use of a position of power or trust over another person to induce them to enter into a contract against their free will (Section 16, Indian Contract Act, 1872).

Unlawful Consideration: Consideration that is forbidden by law, is fraudulent, causes injury to a person or property, is immoral, or is opposed to public policy. A contract with unlawful consideration is void.

This glossary is not exhaustive, but it covers many of the essential terms used in basic contract law. Understanding these terms can empower individuals to engage more confidently in legal agreements.

About the Author

Siva Prasad Bose is an author and legal writer who has authored more than twenty introductory guidebooks on aspects of Indian laws in both Hindi and English. His books are designed to make complex legal topics accessible to general readers, students, and professionals across India. He is a retired officer of Uttar Pradesh Power Corporation Limited, where he served for many years in a technical and administrative capacity. He holds an engineering degree from Jadavpur University, Kolkata, a law degree (LL.B.) from Meerut University, Meerut, and a Bachelor of Science degree from MMH College, Ghaziabad. His areas of special interest include family law, civil law, contract law, electricity law, and revenue law. His books are published by Joy Bose and are available on major e-book and print-on-demand platforms.

His interests lie in the fields of family law, civil law, law of contracts, and areas of law related to electricity generation and revenue related issues.

Other Books by Siva Prasad Bose

Introduction to Wills and Probate

Senior Citizens Abuse in India

Introduction to Negotiable Instruments

Introduction to Marriage Laws in India

Neighbor Problems in India and what to do about them

Managing Court Cases with Mental Strength

Delays in Court Cases in India

Self-Publish Books and E-Books in India

Introduction to Patents and Patent Law in India

Introduction to Property Law in India

Don't miss out!

Visit the website below and you can sign up to receive emails whenever Siva Prasad Bose publishes a new book. There's no charge and no obligation.

https://books2read.com/r/B-A-RVCN-BNGYB

BOOKS 2 READ

Connecting independent readers to independent writers.

Did you love *Introduction to Contract Law in India*? Then you should read *Introduction to Marriage Laws in India*[1] by Siva Prasad Bose!

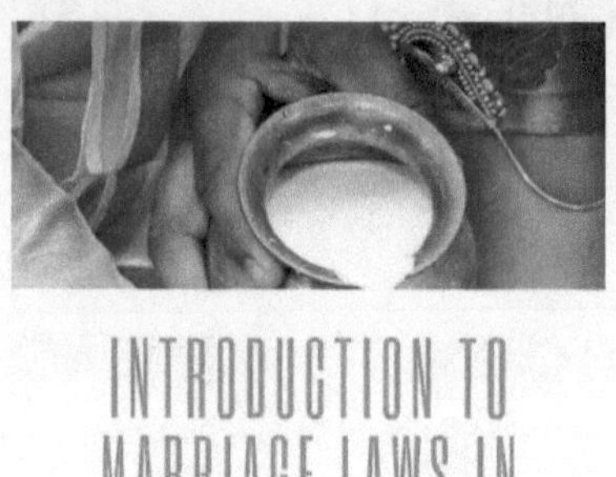

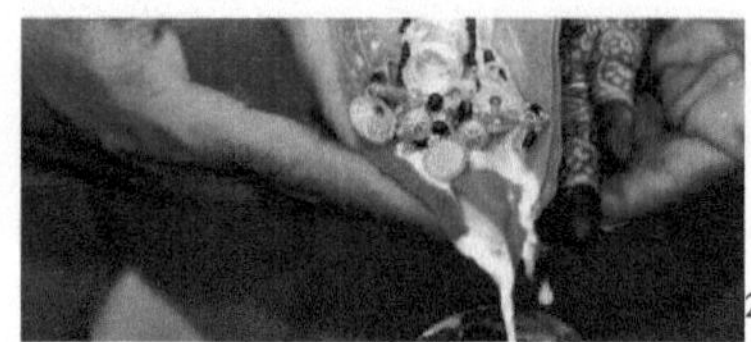

Marriage laws form a vital pillar of India's legal system — and understanding them has never been more important. With divorce rates rising rapidly among India's new generation and matrimonial disputes becoming increasingly common, knowing your legal rights and obligations within a marriage is essential knowledge for every Indian citizen.

Written in plain, accessible language for the non-lawyer, this practical guide cuts through legal complexity to give readers a clear, comprehensive understanding of how Indian marriage law works — from the moment a marriage is solemnized to the legal processes that follow if it breaks down.

---

1. https://books2read.com/u/3R66rB

2. https://books2read.com/u/3R66rB

What You Will Learn

This book covers the full landscape of Indian matrimonial law, including what makes a marriage valid under the Hindu Marriage Act and Special Marriage Act, the legal distinction between void and voidable marriages, and the full range of grounds for divorce — from adultery and cruelty to desertion and mental disorder. Readers will find step-by-step guidance on contested divorce and mutual consent divorce, an explanation of judicial separation and restitution of conjugal rights, and a clear account of how courts approach mental cruelty through landmark judgments. The book also covers domicile and jurisdiction, division of property and streedhan, and two of the most widely invoked laws in matrimonial disputes — Section 498a and the Domestic Violence Act. The full text of the Hindu Marriage Act, 1955 is included as an appendix for easy reference.

Whether you are preparing for marriage, facing a matrimonial dispute, supporting a family member through a difficult separation, or simply seeking to understand your legal rights, this book gives you the foundational knowledge you need — without requiring a law degree to understand it.

Read more at https://sivaprasadbose.wordpress.com/.

About the Author

Siva Prasad Bose is an electrical engineer by profession. He is currently retired after many years of service in Uttar Pradesh Power Corporation Limited. He received his engineering degree from Jadavpur University, Kolkata and has a law degree from Meerut University, Meerut. His interests lie in the fields of family law, civil law, law of contracts, and any areas of law related to power electricity related issues.

Read more at https://sivaprasadbose.wordpress.com/.